Dawn's Lament

Adrian Clark

BookLeaf
Publishing

Presentation by *BookLeaf Publishing*

Web: www.bookleafpub.com

E-mail: info@bookleafpub.com

ISBN: 9789357213882

First edition 2023

*To the forgotten and the buried, I piece myself
back together at dawn for you. I wonder if this
will ever make it into your hands.*

Umbra |
escape

I hold the night sky's silence in my mouth, feeling it trickle down my chin as it slips away from me, washed from my mouth by the absence of the words I am too afraid to say. The gentle spring air sings beneath the moonlight, rustling the leaves under beams of starlight. I feel it in all its tenderness between the small of my back; no matter how hard I try I cannot seem to breathe it in. Do you know what that is like, to have the whole world pressed upon your forehead, to hear it beckon you in the darkness and be unable to step inside? My lungs ache for a breath of love, to live all the lives I am ready to start living. This heavy feeling does not belong in my chest, my toes, my fingers; it nuzzles up beside me at night and I know I do not wish to be in these shadows. I have been plucking petals from a rose and yet that too leaves me with more questions than answers.

Porta Caeli |
fractures; first mend

I

Farewell waved to the window of frost;
(Why must it be goodbye?)
Gone from sight you disappear,
I lay on the floor with my eyes to the ceiling
(My vision remains blurry my dear)
Heaven's door looms so brightly above me,
I can feel it kissing the tip of my nose
beckoning me closer still.
(Despair blankets me so heavily
I forgot to breathe.)

II

Beg again to the moon shining above,
perhaps she can stop this aching in my chest;
(This agony manifests a sadness in my soul
I must take another breath.)
yesterday's stars are shining above,
your face still lingering by the doorway in my
sleep.

(What of those nights of fluttering words,
Love dancing in the air between us?)

Cordolium |
in wilted flowers I lie

I'm sick of all these colors that dance at the edge of my vision / when I lock my eyes to yours / your smile chains me / with its gentle beckoning nature / I cannot seem to shake you from my bones / kerosene and flames / a moth drops to their death; falling ashes fly by my face and I roar with laughter / a maniacal smile plastered upon me / must my sins bubble and flow over the sunrise in an all-black glory? / they seem to ignite within me whenever that ember starts in my chest once more / a spiral of regret that only pulls me further in when my feet stumble far too close to the edge / ravens circle above patient in their descent / this will tear me apart / they flap their wings and bark their melancholic staccatos / soon they shall swoop / the wounds inflicted upon my bared heart as I tumble through open air / blood filled with burning agony / my hands ache from all the memories I have lost when their back turned towards me / forgive me / my chest tightens at the thought of what this feels like / it is time for you to walk away.

Praestigriae |
abyssal; edge of the world

Heavy is my head, filled with smog and wisps of
dreams unheard; a crown of shadows lays upon
my brow, obsidian thorns burrowing into my
temples with no escape in sight. I am losing
myself to this madness, this lingering feeling of
inescapable dread; I fear the pits that I fall into
when the mirror reflects the shadows under my
skin. I am drowning in a pool of my own doing,
an inescapable torrent of regrets pouring from
every crevice in my ever cracking facade, slowly
saturating me in the darkness that has always
loomed over these tired bones. I wonder who
shall steer these reins, as this chariot of gold
teeters on the edge of the Abyss. It is taking all
my willpower not to tip myself forward into the
darkness; he beckons me into his domain of
black flames, temptation saturating the ends of
my trembling fingertips. Perhaps the pain will
revive me.

Angelus |
fallen at dawn

I am not one to tell you how to breathe, or what path you are meant to walk with those tired feet of yours. Today, we are of the sky, tomorrow we shall be the earth itself. The air of summer gone ruffles your hair shining in the light. Will you ever leave? You belonged not to me, but to your own pride and greed; a vice greater than any of the dreams I tried to contain you in. I wanted to join you, up above where the world seemed so much sweeter. It seems to me the feathers plucked out of my back were your doing in the end. I wish to have known you, upon this scorching earth where love is swallowed in desperation; in another existence perhaps you were meant to hold my heart. This holds no truth here, where I lay looking up at fallen feathers. As I sink into the beds of camellia and daffodils, I am reminded that the children of the sky were always meant to be free.

Obumbratio |
dazed; madness & the kiss of death

My blood runs cold with the winter chill from that night long ago where my thoughts were not my own. I drove horrors into my own skin, jagged edges of the mirror staring back at me from the floor. Is this what pain is supposed to make me feel? I wanted to rip it out of my spirit and place it onto this empty body of mine. I inflicted agony upon you haven't I, my love? Those flashes of red haunt me when I toss and turn in my sleep. I unraveled myself when this vermillion cloak overtook me, tugged upon the fraying string till I felt myself choking on the earth. You were in the crossfire, between my wrists and the blades I kept hidden in my pocket. Your cries of anguish forever haunt my dreams, where I sat atop a snowy hill with silver gleaming in my hands. I still feel your arms cradling my head when the voices get too loud. I regret letting you see me destroy myself like I did. I deserved nothing but the grave I was digging myself. You should have thrown me off the edge, my blackened angel of mercy; I was not worthy of being loved by you, not in those dark hours.

Noctem |
to love is to yield

Some nights are sewed into the back of my eyes, held in the hours of dawn when my bedside lay empty. I am always reminded of the night under the setting sun, that embrace of a lost world etched into my skin like the scars of a wildfire. Our love was the temporary kind, the one where even our heartbeat paused to hold its breath in fear of losing the moment. How long did we sit there, my love? I lost time to the shaking of your hands. A farewell heavy with the unsaid, in my heart I knew that you were not meant to be held. You with your jagged edges and tongue of sweet nothings. The sun is not one to yield, to sit in the quiet that stillness can bring. You are too bright for this world, this cacophony of greed and hatred that saturates the horizon. You were meant to burn your own path, you and your fiery heart of gold and ash. I should have let you be, to blaze on through daylight's reign; instead I lay scorched upon this earth, dazed and stricken with loathing.

Mania |
Thursday, September 1. |
11:12am
soaring flames, slumber—

I think I fell off the edge. My room seems
empty.

Where did my smile
go?
I think it ran to fetch my mind. It scurried away
in fear of itself. Likely to unravel the crimson
threads that lay unspooled on the floor.
Am I in a dream?
I think the stars are failing me. They have started
to fall once more. Autumn has come again and
my chest feels empty. Summer's end has always
brought my own heart on a platter littered with
ashes. I inhale this smoke the way I grabbed
your hand just the other day. Fervently and
without restraint. Your voice echoes in the
hollowness within me.

I shall never wake up.
These memories will always haunt me. They
creep up on me when my hands tremble like
they do. I do not know if I can escape you. Your

laughter still lurks around dark corners. Did
shadows peek through my cracks, too?
Am I in a dream?

Adolescentia | innocence; partner of plethora

In my youth I knew this girl
Whose smile carried me with her
Drifting upon the winds of winter nights.

The world opened to me
It is then my heart bloomed
With love like summer rain
Drenching me in the golden light of dawn's kiss.

Happiness finally made a home of me
Breaking these walls of onyx
That encased this heart of steel and ice
Her gentle glow enveloped me
Burning to reveal the gold underneath.

She shall never be erased
From skin nor dreams
The first is always the purest
Magnified by the naivety of youth
Although it ran its course far too quickly
My heart searches for someone like her once
more.

Vereri |
prayer; springtime glutton

Golden light beams from between our interlocked fingers and I cannot help but feel that this was meant to be. You are all I have ever wished for, my love. My pulse quickens at the sound of my name on your lips, the grazing of your fingers igniting a flame that burns me anew. Every dream I have contains your name hidden within. This love consumes me in a way where I cannot help but cower to the enormity of it. In this world of chaos and greed and loss and emptiness, you have been a healing light for this mending soul of mine. I shall kiss those calloused fingertips if only in repentance for the chaos swirling within me; by the grace of all things good, I felt happiness finally seep into my skin when your presence made a home for me.

Monimentum |
a grave

Haunting memories of the past plague me,
yet still love prevails in its eternal nature;
that which radiates cannot be extinguished
in its entirety.

Shine as it may,
here it lays to rest,
in the cemetery for words
that were almost beautiful enough to breathe.

Almost, but not quite yet.

Nativus |
kintsugi; a moment of repair

I may think of your name softly from time to
time, when I hear the rustling of leaves and see
the way the sky turns crimson after an autumn
day. How I have yearned for ecstasies long gone,
on this day where love was murmured in my ear
for the first time. How can I look at that time
without remembering the magic of the moment?
Wandering hands and sly smiles, soft whispers
of futures not yet found; naivety born blind by
hopes and delusion. Time has not been kind to
my heart, tugging me waywardly past flower
shops and benches where sunsets waned for us.
My cracks are filled with gold, an attempt to
hide the horrors that sit upon my skin from the
hurts of you. It is days like this on a dreary
afternoon that I am filled with hazy thoughts,
missing happy memories. Even though your face
is blurry now, I wonder sometimes who we
could have been; if life was not so cruel and if
our hearts were a little bit older.

Exlecebra |
finality; fate's farewell

You were but a love for a season
A burning crusade of greed and hurt
Amplified only by the sun's rays.

A break in daylight's path
An echo of a smile only seen under the night sky
Moonlit poison falling from the mirror.

Love lies within moon charged stones
Under your pillows and on your balcony
I hope they give you everything you need.

Iterum Detegitur |
solitude; seraph

It is that time after dusk when the world stills for
just a breath; all our eternities fall silent as I look
out upon the city, holding my shuddering heart
in my open palm. I have always bled in the name
of love, scarlet thorns etching their songs into
my skin; when you look into my eyes, can you
see how haunted they have become? I have
always had doubt encroaching upon me. I now
ground myself by knowing that my body resides
in this little pocket of stars my bones fill up; a
home I am still trying to build of my body.
Hushed whispers float around me, telling me I
have a place in this withering world, of fire and
passion and greed. I am learning to find pieces
of joy in meaning something at all, in a world
where everyone wants to mean something to
someone; chasing love around dark corners,
hoping one day it falls into my lap wrapped with
a pretty bow. It is in this moment where I
remember that I can be enough for myself too,
me and the stars and the flowers that bloom in
the moonlight.

Omnia Vincit Amor | serendipity; a love lost; contrition

Regret always permeates my bones when your name enters my thoughts. Many loves have left me, but your absence left scars that have stood the test of time. You were sent to show me kindness in the world and I threw it all away for the man that shattered me, time and time again. My ghost clawed his way back to me and I held his hand instead of yours; it will take me the rest of my life to accept the mistake of leaving you for empty promises. I know not why I let myself be torn apart, baring my heart to destruction with open arms; had I let you love me the way you did, this book would have written itself with happiness rather than sorrow. Not a day goes by without my soul aching for yours. The death of my heart was no fault but my own. You will always be my angel, etched onto my arm in the shape of a sword and moon. That invocation was murmured in your name, the sword of eternality bequeathed upon me by the purity in your soul.
 I ran away from you, who could have been my greatest love;

there will always be a place for you here beside me, if somehow these words reach you.

Incendium |
perish; the tide; reflection &
realization

My desires know not of these calloused fingers. I grip the edge of the water so furiously, praying that you would make its way back to me. Bruises bloom upon my knees where I knelt in supplication, begging for love lost to the rippling tide. They told me love falters under an abundance of light, fading when the sun burns too brightly; I suppose I must find acceptance behind my gritted teeth, all these years later. My heart knows no bounds, consuming myself until I found a seat upon this cracked earth. I have left myself here, scrying through the moonlit pool hoping for a glimpse of a future far beyond our reach now. Between the crossroads of yearning and mourning, the death of us was laid to rest. I must sit here for a while, staring into the reflection of your smile in the water. Forget about me, my love. You are safer in my memories.

Aeternus |
forever; imprinted

I still see pieces of you in my car
where your laughter still rings in my ears;
your presence lingers where I lay my head to
rest, blurry moments of us still live on
behind closed eyes.

Little did I know
your memories would scatter themselves,
encroaching on the edges of my world
begging to be let in again;
sunlight through a morning window.

My heart has found a home in every chest but
my own, as if my own body will not contain me;
perhaps I was already born half empty,
with all the loves that I have shared
brushing past like a cool summer breeze.

You are all I love and all I have ever loved
you are all the things I wish to cast away
and everything I never wanted.
a piece of me so sacred yet so damned;
will I ever rid myself of the beauty of you?

Lux Brumalis |
erato; burning crescendo; bared

My hands have started to shake with the future [phantom pains from the caress of your fingers] [this feeling is familiar yet all too different for me to grasp]. I am wondering when this gap shall close [jump with me over this abyss, will you?], my heart pounds in my chest till it feels like it will burst [starlight escapes when your name enters my thoughts]. There is an unsaid yearning in these veins that I do not know how to show you [my words live in my dreams, stuck in my throat far too long]; how do I tell you there is a place for you here, next to me? It lives between the pages of this book we share [will it have a happy ending?], where I hope we live on with its memories. My head stays drifting, between what can be and how to get there; this peace is something I wish to hold onto [take my hand, please?].

Vespera |
uada; the mark of sin;
incineration

I

I am not made for this world, of vice and chains beyond the light's reach; I must return back to the ways of darkness that lick my heels, those eyes threaded with temptation. The calls of fury sound through the air where despair gives way to cries of defeat, falling into the land of denied salvation through the cracks in these trembling, cupped palms. Repentance staves away only so much, when shadows lurk around every corner; crimson storms and the death of dreams flow through these veins of aurum and moonlight. So here I lay upon this blackening horizon. Where the allure of endless nothingness takes hold of me, a chokehold of air long left.

II

This treacherous demise settles upon these sunken shoulders, mania tracing my skin in its conquest. The edge beckons to me, you know. I fear the simplicity in turning towards the looming monsters that caress my back. They have sat in waiting since I dove into the pools of sunlight, where I wished to be cleansed of these lingering tendrils. Yet sin tastes so sweet when it wraps itself around my throat and I have welcomed its presence with open arms; there is a futility of struggling against its pull and so I bathe in its glory. One day, when the flames die down from the edges of my vision, I will find my salvation. The light shall reach for me from another galaxy, another time; I shall be there soon my dear, when I must leave myself as ashes blowing in the summer wind.

www.ingramcontent.com/pod-product-compliance
Lightning Source LLC
Chambersburg PA
CBHW070734160726
48003CB00006BA/2508